DIG A MOAT, BUILD A CASTLE

DIG A MOAT, BUILD A CASTLE

Six Things Great Companies Do that You Should Too

GOKUL PADMANABHAN

CONTENTS

Introduction 1
Remain Customer Centric 5
Play Financial Offense 11
Maintain a Profit-First Perspective 15
Embrace the Owner Mindset 21
Develop Engaged & Satisfied Employees 28
Uphold Your Bold Vision, Mission & Purpose 34
Conclusion 37

INTRODUCTION

If you've picked up this book, chances are you're a small business owner, like me. You've built, or are in the process of building, your business and have met with some large successes and a challenge or two. Business ownership is a personal journey. You're in the trenches making the important decisions that will continue to impact your bottom line as well as the lives of others. There's a constant balance of risk and reward, investment and return, time spent versus benefit earned.

As brokers specific to the restoration space, my team and I are in a very unique spot, watching as owners like you build successful businesses that are contributors to the industry. We look at companies and talk to owners from all over the country. It's the nature of our business. From our vantage point, we have a bird's eye view into what's working and what's not.

I see P&Ls and financials come across my desk each day. We witness the nitty gritty of how businesses run internally—thousands of financial documents, hundreds of businesses, and some very key strategies that point to the difference between success and what marks murky waters ahead for a business.

Every now and then I'll talk to an owner, review the workings of the company, and say, "WOW!" Sadly, those are rare finds. Quality companies are often the exception, not the rule.

For years, as I've studied these companies, I've found myself scratching my head and wondering, "what's the difference?"

The answer is as complex as it is simple—on-purpose companies know what they're doing and why they're doing it.

WHAT'S AN ON-PURPOSE COMPANY, YOU ASK?

- It's a business where employees understand the vision and mission clearly and have no doubt about their role in realizing that vision.
- It's an owner that's engaged and taking intentional, planned action to move the business forward.
- It's the easy-to-say but hard-to-implement bits that we, as business owners, often overlook in our focus to get the day-to-day work done.

- It's doing the hard things consistently, until they're no longer hard.

Rinse. Wash. Repeat. We continue to live this message. We speak it and do it, every single day, so that we don't lose touch with the important aspects of our business.

When I speak to business owners about what it takes to succeed in owning a restoration business and really become one of those top 5% performers, I always start with this:

DIG A MOAT & BUILD A CASTLE.

The response is precisely what you'd think, a few raised eyebrows and a whole lot of questions. When we take a step back, the concept is simple. We're all small businesses trying to be really good at doing what we do.

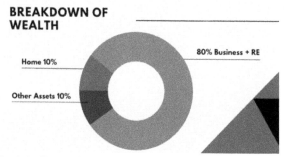

Statistically, small business owners in the United States have close to 80% of their wealth tied into their business and the business real estate. If this is the case, then success is vital.

To establish yourself in your industry, you must set yourself apart from others (digging a moat). The pieces of your business that differentiate you become your moat, your protection from competition. It's only once you've created this construct to protect your business that you can begin building that castle, that empire, that best business that performs high above others in the industry.

In almost two decades helping restoration owners sell their businesses, the message of what makes a business successful has become clear. Creating a quality business that will perform, grow, and leave a legacy requires six foundational principles. In these pages, I've laid out the six things all great companies do that you should too.

1
REMAIN CUSTOMER CENTRIC

In business ownership, as in life, people are always looking for the next shiny thing, and I'm here to tell you it's immaterial. Delighting your customers to grow your business is the same today as it was 100 years ago. The fundamentals of the game never change. Sometimes we have to stop searching for those magic formulas and get back to basics – block and tackle – fundamentals.

Good businesses are extremely customer-centric and built around the customer. There's no doubt about it. As brokers, we see people at all stages of business, and showing up with our customers as our priority is about the little things and the connection. In business, you connect before you convert.

There's always a tendency to rush to the technical side, but the customer-centric companies are caring first. They connect first and develop that high trust. Out of that foundation, anything is possible. Whether you're responding to a communitywide disaster or approaching a large loss, the way you connect with each customer and interact with them matters—every time. It's the little things that cost nothing.

In a world of tech, cloud-based systems and automation, people are starving for connection. Sadly, the bar is no longer high, and we need to sit in that. People are desperate for someone to shake their hand and tell them they care. Your goal is more than to provide service; it's to wrap each customer in a blanket of compassion and give them what I call the *chicken noodle soup treatment.*

All incredibly meaningful advances in your business come through connection. If an owner says, "I wish I could run a business without customers," I know that business is not sellable, because it's not based in connection. There's no reason for them to exist. I don't need to look at those financials—I know where that business is landing.

CASE STUDY

When I bought my pool screen contracting business seven years ago, we had a 2.2 rating on Google. People thought of customers as a problem. Every job was just another customer, just another project. The company looked at jobs as addresses, not as the people on the other end of the phone.

Right away we got to work implementing changes that would improve our customer service and shift our team's mindset and approach to their work. I placed a big board in the warehouse hallway where I began tracking all customer feedback—compliments, negative comments, and putbacks (mistakes on the jobs that needed to be fixed). Customer satisfaction became a pillar upon which our business was built. I wanted to know the why behind the good, the bad, and everything in between.

As the reviews were posted on Fridays, I'd watch employees walk down the hallway slowly, looking at what they saw. It got so that technicians would see anything under a five-star review posted for one of their jobs and be at my office door, ready to discuss before I brought them in for a talk. Accountability was key.

Quality customer service became a priority. It was at the epicenter of our business, and we were intent on transforming the customer experience. We committed to getting positive feedback, and to do that, we had to dissect every issue and see what we could do better.

Owners who make customer satisfaction part of their success strategy have the best litmus test for success and can easily work backward to diagnose the concerns that come up. At my pool screen business, as we turned our focus to creating the best customer experience, online customer ratings went from 2.2 to 4.3 in just over a year.

It absolutely transformed the business. The more happy customers we had, the more sales grew, and the more we could reduce our marketing budget. It was a win across the board.

RESTORATION PERSPECTIVE

One of the biggest complaints in this industry is the lack of communication as companies continue to overpromise and underdeliver. It's important to be big on overcommunicating the good, the bad, and the ugly. If the permit department says four months to get a permit, promise five. Help the customer understand the expectation and avoid being a "yes man."

One of the simplest and most effective ways to communicate during a project is through well-executed progress reports for each job. When you communicate what you've done each week and your goals for the following week, you can help your customers understand the process and be invested during what often amounts to a high-stress situation.

Moreover, when you can show substantial progress from week to week, the client has buy-in and can watch progress as it occurs. It's important not to hide from bad news.

The key to quality customer experiences begins with assigning a single point of contact between the company and the client. This may be a project manager or a marketing, sales, or customer service rep. When a handoff to a different member of the team is required, it must be very clear and well executed.

At every vital touchpoint of the customer journey, scripts should be in place to address common questions, basic information, and troubleshooting scenarios for common situations. When the entire team follows your script, the process is clear, and communication is uniform.

When it comes to bonuses and additional compensation for your team members, tying it to customer feedback can change the game. The right team facilitates the best customer experience, and their compensation should reflect those wins that benefit the company.

QUESTIONS TO CONSIDER

- Do you follow up and follow through with past clients?
- Do you have an automated process to get customer feedback?
- Do you prioritize customer feedback in your daily operations?

2
PLAY FINANCIAL OFFENSE

Understanding your finances and the numbers that indicate a healthy, successful business is something top performers prioritize in every scenario. To run a business to its fullest potential, you must have a high-level understanding of financial reporting, margins, and profits.

Great companies look at each job independently to determine the revenue, profitability, and its impact on the business as a whole. When you understand the language of accounting, when you can read a WIP report and discuss GAAP principles, then you are better equipped to look to the future of your business and how the present is affecting your success.

The discipline you exhibit in keeping your books will inform every aspect of your business, and engaging an outsourced, objective bookkeeper or hiring a CFO gives you the distance to make decisions while keeping eyes on the books at all times. You must be in the habit of looking at your books regularly. At the end of the day, your success will show up in the revenue per employee, a metric that top performing businesses keep top-of-mind.

CASE STUDY

Let's say you are running a business at $3.2 million in revenue with 22 or 23 employees. This breaks down to a revenue of $130,000 per employee. Your margins will be a lot less if you run the same business with more employees. Revenue per employee is one of the most important numbers you should keep track of when scaling your business.

Over 50% of the owners we work with do not understand their EBITDA. Everybody's running their business out of a checkbook. It's like going to the eye doctor for a headache – it doesn't tell you anything substantial about your business.

You've got to run your business out of P&L's – not your checkbook. I see large companies ($20-30 million in revenue) where owners have no clue where they are in their business, and that can mean the difference between a company that serves others and a company that is destined for something other than success.

It's one of the toughest calls I make every week. Every Friday I set aside time for customer recovery, which means calling clients to tell them the bas news, that their business is unprofitable or unsellable. Telling someone who's ready to sell their business that the business is not as sellable as they think is just the worst part of my job, especially since it's a piece that is avoidable when building a business. Things like this affect people in big ways.

RESTORATION PERSPECTIVE

We get so busy with the hammer and nails part of our business, and we have to become really aware that our role as owners of the business is not the hammer and nails bit; it's to dig a moat and build a castle.

You start by learning very basic accounting principles, because accounting is the language of business.

You must, at minimum, understand the following:

- P&Ls
- Balance Sheets
- Cashflow
- Revenue per Employee

QUESTIONS TO CONSIDER

- What was your revenue per employee last year versus this year?
- How can you increase revenue per employee?
- Block 90 minutes every Friday morning to review your financials, with your bookkeeper or accountant or by yourself.

3
MAINTAIN A PROFIT-FIRST PERSPECTIVE

Let's not beat around the bush. Your business is here to make a profit. Successful businesses function on key performance tenets: take care of employees; take care of customers; and make a profit.

If you don't make a profit, you can't fulfill the other two. You're either a CEO or not, and people are going to do their job or they're not. What you do with that can be generous, but it's got to start with that simple concept, in all decisions and action plans.

An unprofitable company is not doing anything for anyone. I've never seen the Apple CEO called anything else or the president of a large successful company called something else. You bear a big responsibility to those in your business, and without a profit-minded approach, no one wins.

Here's what I find great companies and entrepreneurs are focused on. It's about profit and being able to do good things with it in your community. It's amazing how many owners are focused on things other than the reason they exist in the first place, their prime directive—to serve clients and employees and create a profit.

These concepts are not just theories sitting in a book. They're key success strategies we have gleaned from studying the industry. Putting them into practice can make or break a business in the restoration space.

In a single quarter, we talked to 104 owners at different levels of ownership. 94 of them weren't ready to sell, and it's because they're not focused on profits.

Sure, we'll advise those clients and give them a roadmap for change, or they'll hang up because they're backed into a corner. If you're consistently working on digging a moat and building your castle, you'll be ready and profitable.

I've had the pleasure of sitting down with two great friends and top experts in the industry to discuss this very idea. Recently, I sat down on my podcast with Scott Miller, and later with Phil Rosebrook, to get their insights on the importance of creating profitable businesses. We discussed, at length, the importance of setting goals and budgets by project.

- When you completely understand a profit-first mindset, every employee and team works to their capacity.
- When teams are not working at capacity, your margins erode.
- When your time goals and schedules aren't compressed to keep projects moving, the profit potential degrades.
- Looking at each job as its own vessel and scrutinizing one job at a time really does matter, and that's how the great companies stay ahead.
- If you're not planning your time, supplies, subcontractors, budgets, and schedules to optimize your profit, then all of a sudden, you're missing supplies, something as simple as a board, and you're wandering off to Home Depot to get that board, leaving behind the important work that needs done and setting your project back.

Great companies run every job by monitoring the metrics of that specific job. Poor work habits compound, and without accountability and close monitoring of well-planned and executed schedules, budgets, and teams, leaky holes appear in your systems and erode your project. A team with the right plan and the oversight to execute it is doing exponentially more jobs each year, affecting the bottom line in important ways.

CASE STUDY

A year or so ago, I was working with a business that was highly revenue focused, not profit focused. The business had $4 million in revenue. For most of its 38 years in business, the owner focused on revenue.

I sat down with the owner, and we went through each project, discussing how we could plan them out to be more profit oriented. We decided each project must have minimum requirements for gross margins, and that very simple process of planning things led to a standard, master process that was duplicated for all other projects.

By the time his business was ready to sell, his revenue had taken a small dip, but his profit margins had increased by close to 60%. Understanding the importance of profit brings clarity beyond the revenue number.

When you're profit focused, you're cutting out what doesn't serve your bottom line and making the tough decisions that you've avoided, all while celebrating those high revenue reports. Ultimately, your business operating at optimum profit is more successful and likely more scalable.

RESTORATION PERSPECTIVE

Profit-driven business mindset is a struggle in any industry but specifically in restoration. It's important to have a CFO and make sure you're keeping an eye on financials so there are no surprises. Sit down with your CFO once a month and make sure everything looks good.

Keep a close eye on expenses, and you'll be shocked at how much can be done with a small workforce that's working smartly. Drive revenue numbers up and keep overhead low and don't forget your bottom line in every aspect of your business.

One of the big things people don't talk about is the ability to negotiate. Be as lean as possible and ask for discounts wherever you can get them. Pennies and dimes add up, and they matter more than what people think.

Your focus should be on monitoring your bottom line and your profitability. It's easy to get distracted by the shiny, bright revenue numbers and forget the most important piece of the financial puzzle.

If you're not making money, then the meaning behind what you're doing diminishes. Study the revenue generated by each employee to see contributions per employee and get a better understanding of how much each employee must generate with their efforts for the company to stay profitable. This puts the bigger picture into perspective.

QUESTIONS TO CONSIDER

- Are you looking at your financials (P&Ls and balance sheets) weekly to track profits?
- Do you have a professional bookkeeper or dedicated employee that keeps your books?
- Do you understand how much your business needs to earn to be profitable and take care of your employees and customers?

4

EMBRACE THE OWNER MINDSET

In business ownership it's vital to avoid burnout and disengagement. High performance organizations have an owner who's no more than 1% engaged in the day-to-day and has the mindset to go with that.

It's important to break down that mindset and fully understand it. As the leader of the company, the CEO, the person in charge, your job is one thing – dig a moat; build a castle.

Digging the moat requires getting your differentiation, value proposition, and customer service so locked in that no competition can ever come and raid your castle. Building a castle means establishing your business empire and your profits. The CEO has to focus on profits. That's the job. Without profits, there's nothing else.

The answers you get in your mind depend on the questions you ask. Ask different questions for different answers. Then, you'll find opportunities everywhere. It's an exercise in shifting your mindset.

Building a business requires growing into the different job descriptions and mindsets at every stage of the company's development.

RAINMAKER: When you start a business, you're a rainmaker, making those sales because it's important. At the start, you're a one-man operation, maybe working out of a van without a brick and mortar. You're all about sales. That's your job description – to bring sales in the door. This startup phase is a time when bringing in clients and generating business is key. You're laying the foundation for big things to come.

TEAMBUILDER: You're now a year or two into your business, and you're adding a person here and there, maybe moving to a facility with decent square footage, ready to establish your team. People who are really good rainmakers may not naturally be team builders, but good business owners learn to transition into their job description and get good at it. You're building a team with some trucks, a warehouse. Your job description has changed, and you must acquire the skills to put a successful team in place.

SYSTEMIZER: Once you're growing, you need to systemize, if you want the same performance over and over and over. The right team and the right systems are helping sustain your success and grow your business strategically. As they gel, everything begins to run on KPIs, and production is improving. Your revenue per employee is growing and healthy.

INVESTOR: As you become a proficient systemizer, your business continues to grow. 10% growth for a really big company is phenomenal, and as you grow, your job description changes again to an investor or CEO. You are digging your moat and building your castle. You're looking at your business from financials and internal rate of growth, squeezing more juice out of every dollar.

ARCHITECT: At this point in your business, you can either stay to become an architect and look at expanding your territory, services, verticals, etc. or choose to sell. If you are stuck as an investor, your business will plateau. When you become an architect, you're positioned to scale and eventually exit your business.

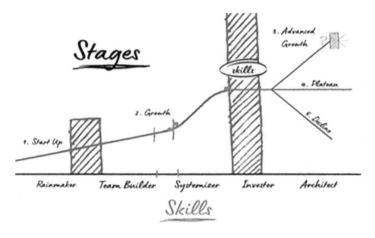

Successful owners are always growing along with the business, and the business never grows beyond the owner. Mindset is so important in the owner role, from rainmaker to architect. We've sold businesses that have been in the market for 30+ years and whose owners have a mindset that the market is saturated and their time for growth is over. Inevitably, a new business owner comes in and triples the revenue. Why? Mindset.

CASE STUDY

You may not have started your business digging a moat and building a castle, but now you're invested, empowered, and making sure you're protecting your legacy. You're making sure no one can come in and raid that castle. You've got replacement staff and such great connections in your area/city that it doesn't matter if a national player buys one of your competitors or drops an office next to you.

No one can attack that castle. Maybe your inner marketing has been great for years and you're hyper-local and dominating, not just with ads, but content, commitment, and contribution to the community. It doesn't matter if someone comes in with a $10 million budget – they're never replacing those connections.

You look at your talent and team and keep them happy. The best part? You are only as good as the people on the field, and great talent is what you're building around your firm. Great talent fends off what's coming at you – along with the right skills and knowledge.

Differentiate yourself. Then, your competitor is you versus you. You're competing with yourself to up your own game instead of embracing that mindset of competition and scarcity. If you become a true CEO Investor and embrace that job description, you'll only be thinking about how to dig a moat and build a castle. The rest will just be noise.

RESTORATION PERSPECTIVE

What is the difference between the respectful leader and the fearful leader?

When your team sees you as a part of the unit, a respectful leader, the game changes. Being involved in the business without inserting yourself in the day-to-day can be executed with mindfulness and attention to your company's needs.

If anything, it can make you more available to support your team while driving the business forward. Fearful leadership does not engage team members or foster loyalty, and in the restoration space a loyal, functioning team is required to succeed.

When we work alongside people, not in front of them, we get the best possible results to move forward. Choose the right people. It's not about being above your team. It's about the mindset that employees respond to. When a team works together towards a single goal that must be accomplished, there is no star player, there is only a cohesive group.

QUESTIONS TO CONSIDER

- Do you have a strong value proposition in place that differentiates your business?
- Are you running the business as an operator or an investor?
- Do you understand what could hold your business back from success?

5

DEVELOP ENGAGED & SATISFIED EMPLOYEES

Companies that treat everyone as adults and seek to have a quality, trusting company culture are rare. High performers are a must. You're only as good as the players on the field, and that requires a mix of different qualities, skill levels, and personality types.

You can't have a full team of Michael Jordans. Every team needs players with different strengths to balance and move the needle forward. It's important to make huge investments in HR and Culture. Family, belonging, attention to team— Covid changed the game here because companies without the right culture could not staff their businesses.

One of the better things that has come out of the past few years is the understanding that our work involves real people who need a clear path forward. That path must include recognition and consideration.

Employee satisfaction is vital. In high-performance companies, team members are reasonably happy and content in their jobs. You don't have to shoot for the moon, but happy employees want to be where they are. Business is so data driven, but we cannot forget that our people are important.

In a high-performance organization, we need everyone moving the ball forward. While holding hands and singing Kumbaya isn't how the world works, employees need that pleasant, enriching experience to remain satisfied.

It's not rocket science, but there's a counterintuitive component to maintaining engaged and satisfied employees. Nothing will bring down employee satisfaction more than a team member who is not performing or who degrades morale.

A lot of owners try to keep and keep and keep and correct and correct and correct, but we need to remove bad apples from our employee roster. It's the quickest way to improve good employee engagement and satisfaction. On the flip side, having bad apples on your team is one of the surest ways to bring down employee satisfaction and engagement.

Many owners make the mistake of hiring employees and telling them what to do. I think the secret to high performance teams is hiring the best people and having them tell YOU what to do. It's a huge characteristic of both high performing teams and employee satisfaction.

CASE STUDY

At RBA, I've carefully selected my team based on their innate strengths, specialized talents, and the contributions they are able to make on a daily basis. Recently, we found ourselves gathering for a team retreat. This is the first in-person gathering for our full group, which includes members from various parts of the country, all working remotely to serve our clients.

During our time together, we did some internal work with the bright and brilliant Mary Tomlinson, one of my dear friends, collaborative partners, and an expert in building on-purpose, synergistic teams.

Together, we participated in an exercise that helped us discover our purpose—both personally and professionally. This purpose was identified in a two-word statement for each team member. The results told us so much about each other and why we bring value to our various positions.

Our admin support and office manager, Lisa, discovered that her purpose is *unearthing treasures*, which perfectly connects the ways she supports our team. Next, we looked at our newest team member and senior client advisor, Jason, whose on-purpose statement is *being true* is devoted to finding the why behind what he does. He supports the team with his willingness and loyalty.

Our most senior client advisor, Bob, was identified as someone who is keen on *imparting wisdom* when he is on purpose. His time and talents are often spent giving information and guidance to team members, clients, and professional partners. Jenny, our Director of Business Development, identified that she is on purpose when she's *affirming significance*—a perfect quality in a person who leads the charge in generating business, forging important industry partnerships, and ensuring a quality customer experience.

My on-purpose statement, you ask? Igniting Joy.

These on-purpose statements are a real quick and dirty way to figure out what makes your team tick, what ignites their passion, and what's going to make them feel unaligned and off-purpose. When you honor your employees and play to their strengths, then you're really building your culture and team.

RESTORATION PERSPECTIVE

People need an opportunity to hear how they're doing and say how they're feeling. Annual reviews and a clear chain of command are important. It's essential to pay good people well and incentivize them for their performance.

You may decide to drive results with profit margin bonuses. A lot of people need to hold their money close to their chest, but in the restoration space, you're not going to keep people if you don't slice the pie more times and build the right bench of key players on your team.

Respect your employees, their opinions, and their contributions, and you'll reap the rewards tenfold with their elevated performance.

SUCCESS DRIVER: OWNER ROLE

REMOVE YOURSELF FROM THE BUSINESS
- You like solving customer problems.
- Nobody know the business like you do.
- The more you are the hub of all activities - the less valuable your company will be.

CONSIDER THE FOLLOWING
- Track your "day in the life." What observations can you make?
- Can current employees expand their role in the business?
- Ask - why do your customers require that you serve them as opposed to your staff?

QUESTIONS TO CONSIDER

- Do you trust your team to make decisions and move your business forward each day without your direct oversight?
- Do you understand each of your employees' strengths, weaknesses, and personal success goals within your business?
- Do your employees have clear assignments, boundaries, and goals that empower them to perform?

6

UPHOLD YOUR BOLD VISION, MISSION & PURPOSE

Everybody has a job to do. More than being accountable to the boss, creating a culture where they're accountable to each other is extremely powerful. There are processes and structures that can be put in place to keep team members accountable to each other. Nothing is more powerful than teams correcting themselves.

Successful CEOs or owners of companies make sure they lay a foundation where peer-to-peer accountability is prevalent, and the team thrives. It's important that the team is not only accountable to you but to themselves and people around them.

Accountability starts at the top. You as an owner are accountable to your team and your company and your customers and stakeholders. Every day, you must step further into your role as CEO to make sure the company is healthy and you're doing all the things you need to be doing. Good or bad, like it or not, your actions filter down into the organization.

RESTORATION PERSPECTIVE

On every project, it's important to trust your team while having the checks and balances in place to verify work. Managing that fine line between holding workers accountable to the team and micromanaging is a constant struggle in an industry where skills are often specialized. Each team member has a role, and they bring their specific skill to the table. With techs, labor, crew supervisors, and other components to every team, it's important to meet on a weekly basis and ensure each team member understands their action items to move their projects forward.

Success comes with proper communication, with building up the team and supporting their efforts. When team members are accountable for their contributions to the team, everyone's voice is heard and the work gets done the right way.

QUESTIONS TO CONSIDER

- Are you a good shepherd of your business (are you motivated every day to grow your business and provide opportunities for your employees)?
- Do you have documented vision, mission, and goals?
- Make a list of all of your employees and rank them from hardest to replace to easiest to replace. Make your contingency plan to keep your bold vision and goals moving forward with the right team.

CONCLUSION

Really great companies are doing fewer things, and they're doing them better. You can have fifty different revenue-generating activities churning away and make very little positive impact on your numbers. The top 5% know how to do three to five things really well and dominate the market.

Understanding your organization's strengths and capacity changes the game. When you're everywhere at once, it's hard to make any meaningful connections, and connection is where the real business takes place.

When you focus on a customer-centric approach to business and have the right systems in place to make fewer unforced errors, you drive revenue. When you put profit first and eliminate what doesn't serve your bottom line, you move the needle forward.

When you're in a success mindset and have engaged, satisfied, and accountable employees, you begin that ascension to the top 5% of business owners in the restoration space, and those are the sellable businesses that are making their mark and setting themselves up for continued future success and growth.

CPSIA information can be obtained
at www.ICGtesting.com
Printed in the USA
JSHW072239160523
41805JS00008B/54

9 781088 135181